Hot Rods

Dennis Pernu

Capstone Press

MINNEAPOLIS

Printed in the United States of America.

Capstone Press • 2440 Fernbrook Lane • Minneapolis, MN 55447

Editorial Director   John Coughlan
Managing Editor   John Martin
Production Editor   James Stapleton
Copy Editor   Thomas Streissguth

Thanks to Ron Drajna for his assistance in the preparation of this book.

Library of Congress Cataloging-in-Publication Data

Pernu, Dennis. 1970--
  Hot rods / by Dennis Pernu
    p. cm. -- (Cruisin')
  Includes bibliographical references and index.
  ISBN 1-56065-253-5 : $13.35
  1. Hot rods--Juvenile literature. [1. Hot rods.
2. Automobiles.] I. Title. II. Series.
TL236.3.P47 1996
629.228--dc20   95-7120
                                                      CIP
                                                      AC

Table of Contents

Chapter 1

What is a Hot Rod?

A hot rod is any car built or altered to meet its owner's needs and tastes. A hot rod is a beautiful and powerful car. Many hot rod owners spend all their extra money **customizing** their special machines. These owners spend months or even years making their hot rod just right. Most **hot rodders** never stop customizing their cars.

Customizing often requires removing **stock** parts from cars. Hot rodders replace these parts with custom parts. A custom part can be a huge new engine. It can also be a tiny **chrome** detail. A hot rodder will spend years looking for the perfect custom parts.

Chapter 2

The History of Hot Rods

In the early 1900s, a Michigan farm boy named Henry Ford invented the assembly line. The assembly line's wheels moved an unfinished car past several workers. As the car rolled by, each worker added a new part.

Henry Ford's workers could build hundreds of cars in a short time. European craftworkers needed a longer time to build just one car. Because Ford's workers built so many cars, Ford was able to sell his cars at a low price. Ford sold 15 million cars by 1930.

Ford's first assembly line had one drawback, however. It produced only one kind of car—the **Model T**. And every one of those Model T's was black.

The First Hot Rods

For most car buyers, the Model T was fine. But others wanted something different. Most people, though, could not afford custom European cars. They customized their black Model T's. Some owners painted their cars different colors. Some bought special equipment that made their Model T's run faster.

The changes owners made reflected their needs and tastes. These early car owners were the first to build hot rods. But the changes made to these Model T's were small compared to what was to come.

Interest in Hot Rods Fades

The Great Depression began in 1929 and ended seven years later in 1936. During that time, there were few jobs. Many people worked for only a few cents an hour. Many young

Customized Model T's were the world's first hot rods.

people could not afford even used cars. There was little interest in customizing cars.

When the Depression ended, young men and women wanted more freedom. The high-speed thrills of automobiles attracted many of them.

Dealers still sold automobiles at a low price. Now nearly anyone could afford a Model T. The even newer **Model A** Fords were rarely more than $50. These **deuce coupes**, as people called the Model A's, were both cheap and reliable.

Many used Model A's were still in excellent condition. These cars became popular among teenagers in the 1930s and 1940s. The deuce

A custom paint job on this 1940s model gives it a lot of flash.

Deuce coupes–Model A Fords–were built for two riders.

coupes were plain and teenagers had to find
ways to make the cars different.

A Hot Rod Pioneer

One of these teenagers was Joe Bailon. The
Depression began when Bailon was in the
second grade. He quit school to work with his
parents in California. They picked fruit and
earned only pennies an hour.

The Depression ended when Bailon was a teenager. Like other teenagers, he liked the cheap Ford roadsters. In 1938, when Bailon turned 16, he bought a 1929 Model A Ford coupe.

Bailon had a wild imagination. He cut off the coupe's cloth roof. He added horns and lights. Then he hand-painted **whitewalls** onto the tires.

Many hot rods carry flames along their sides.

Hot rodders like to build their customized cars close to the ground.

With one more addition, Bailon's custom coupe was complete. He painted flames on the car's nose. This was the first time someone had painted flames on a car. Other young people saw Bailon's wild new ideas. They created new ideas of their own. Joe Bailon's custom coupe helped renew interest in the hot rodding craze.

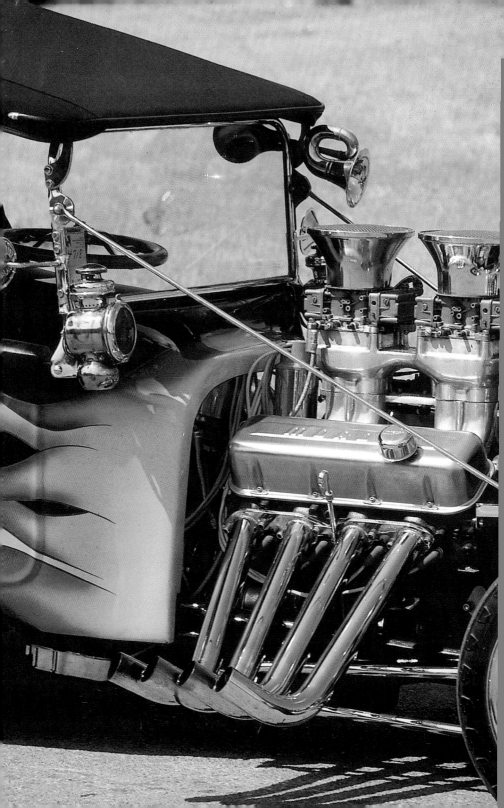

Chapter 3
The Engine

Many hot rodders think the engine is the most important part of the car. It gives the car its power. Some hot rodders hop-up their engines in one of several ways.

Boring the Cylinders

Cylinders are can-shaped parts of an **internal combustion engine**. Gasoline and oxygen are mixed and sucked into the cylinders through **valves**. When a spark ignites this **fuel**, an explosion occurs in each cylinder.

Explosions push the **pistons** downward. The pistons' movement spins the **driveshaft**. The

Chrome engine parts shine under a hot rod hood.

driveshaft turns the rear wheels. When the wheels turn, they push the car forward.

Before 1932, engines had only four cylinders. Hot rodders wanted more speed than **flathead Ford**s could provide.

20

Hot rodders learned to **bore**, or grind, the insides of cylinders. Boring the cylinders makes them larger and causes larger explosions. The extra power of the explosion pushes the pistons faster and spins the driveshaft faster. When the driveshaft spins faster, so do the wheels.

Boring cylinders is not simple. It requires a special tool. Hot rodders who bore their cylinders must be exact. If they grind too much, they may cause the **engine block** to crack. When this happens, the entire engine has to be replaced.

Dual Carburetors

Before the valves suck the fuel into a cylinder, the fuel passes through a **carburetor**. The carburetor mixes the gasoline and air for the engine. If there was no carburetor, the engine might get too much gasoline or air.

To avoid the risks of boring cylinders, a hot rodder might add an extra carburetor. Like larger cylinders, **dual carburetors** allow more gasoline and air into the cylinders.

Superchargers and Fuel Injectors

Another way hot rodders make an engine more powerful is by forcing more fuel into it. Engines with carburetors suck in limited amounts of fuel.

A supercharger or **blower** forces more fuel into the engine. More fuel means bigger explosions in the cylinders.

In the 1950s, some car makers began to build **fuel injectors**. Engines with carburetors or blowers sometimes mix too much gasoline or air into the fuel. A fuel injector injects the correct mixture of fuel a car needs to run efficiently. Most new cars today have fuel injectors instead of carburetors.

Engine Swapping

In 1932, Ford introduced an eight-cylinder engine. This new marvel supplied twice as much power as the small flatheads.

Hot rodders found that these **V-8's** could replace the four cylinders in their Model T's and Model A's. This is how the practice of **engine swapping** began.

Wide back tires are standard equipment on modern hot rods.

In the late 1940s, Cadillac introduced an even more powerful V-8 in its family cars. Hot rodders wanted these powerful engines. They discovered that–with a few extra parts–they could put a Cadillac engine into an old Ford. These hot rods became known as **Fordillacs**.

One of the most powerful of these Cadillac V-8 engines was in the 1949 Mercury. Many

Who needs a hood when you've got solid chrome on the engine block?

hot rodders liked the look of the Mercuries. Instead of putting their engines in old Fords, they **chopped** the Mercury's roof. The chopped

roof gave the cars a sleek and boxy look. Such
cars became known as **Shoebox Fords**.

Over the years, hot rodders learned to swap
more than engines. Today, it is common for a
hot rod to have parts from several different
kinds of cars.

Chapter 4

The Body and Detailing

Only the hot rodder feels the power of the hot rod's engine. The custom paint and details are what everyone else sees.

The Paint Job

A hot rod's paint job is perhaps the most difficult part of customizing. Because everyone sees the outside, the paint job has to be perfect. Many hot rodders hire professionals to paint their machines.

Custom painters complete several steps before they can properly apply paint. First, they completely clean the body. They remove all the rust. If the car is very old, removing the

A convertible hot rod rolls past a crowd of amazed spectators. The owner has pinstriped the sides and detailed his model to perfection.

rust can take days. To skip this step, some hot rodders buy new **fiberglass** bodies. These look exactly like the old bodies.

Custom painters may put dozens of coats of paint on one hot rod. Many times, they often sand each layer by hand before adding a new one.

The two most popular kinds of paint are **metallic** and **pearlescent**. Metallic paint contains tiny chips of metal. When these chips catch the light, the entire car glitters.

Pearlescent paint gives off a deep shine. The shine looks like the rich shiny surface of a pearl.

Detailing

Detailing is important to hot rodders. More than anything else, a car's detailing reflects the owner's personality. Detailing may take the form of a special painted decoration or custom **tuck-and-roll** upholstery. It may be etched-glass windows or handmade wheels.

Joe Bailon's custom flame design in 1938 was one of the first detailing jobs. Since then, flames have been the most popular design among hot rodders. Today, hot rodders decorate their cars in flames of all designs and colors.

Another popular detail is **pinstriping**. Custom painters hand-paint thin lines on cars. These lines often form complicated designs.

Chrome wheels and grille flash from the front end.

One of the most popular details a hot rodder adds is chrome. Hot rodders can buy chrome parts for just about any part of their hot rod. The most obvious chrome parts are the hot rod's wheels. Dealers sell chrome parts for wheels in several styles.

Hot rodders can even add chrome to hidden parts. Hot rodders sometimes buy chrome springs for their suspension systems.

Any part of the engine can be chromed.

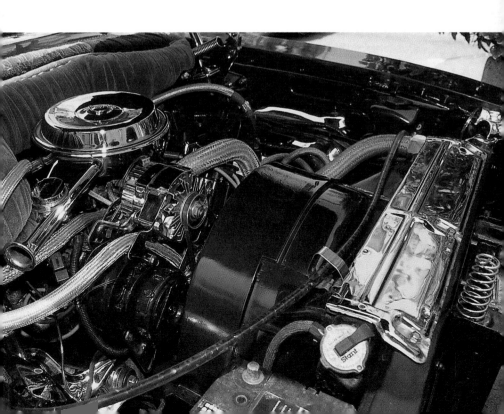

Chapter 5

The Past, Present, and Future of Hot Rodding

Hot rodders have a saying. "In any town where there are two cars, there is bound to be a race." This saying was true in the early days of hot rods. Hot rodders always want to know how to improve their cars. To many, racing their cars seemed the best way to experiment.

In the early days, hot rodders held most of their races on public highways. But those highways were narrow and made of dirt. Many had deep ruts. Racing on them was dangerous to both racers and other motorists. It was also against the law.

SOFT PRETZELS
PIZZA
HOT & DELICIOUS
FOOD
SANDWICHES & FRIES
CONCESSIONS
BY COX
MICHIGAN
SCHOLZ

A Need for Organizations

Hot rodders found safer places to race. They began to form clubs. These clubs met at a dry lake bed west of Los Angeles on Sundays. Club members met to study cars from other clubs, and share their hot-rodding secrets.

The hot rodders also met to race. The sunbaked lake bed was a much safer surface than the narrow dirt highways. Because the lake bed was so far from neighborhoods, hot rodders could make as much noise as they wished.

The SCTA

Unfortunately, there were still a few bad accidents. In the late 1930s, a few hot rodders saw need for safer races. They formed the **Southern California Timing Association (SCTA)**.

The SCTA organized safe and friendly competitions for hot rodders. They recorded the times of the fastest cars. They also held shows in which hot rod clubs could show off the bodies and detailing of their sharpest cars.

Pickup trucks can also be customized.

The SCTA awarded points to the winners of these competitions. At the end of each season, the association named the club with the most points the champion.

The NHRA

Before long, organized drag racing became a popular sport. Hot rodders formed the **National Hot Rod Association** (NHRA) in the 1950s. The NHRA promoted the sport of drag racing across the United States. Today, the NHRA sponsors drag races in dozens of cities.

Muscle Cars

In 1957, the hot rod craze was bigger than ever. That year, General Motors built the famous '57 Chevy. They sold it as a ready-made hot rod.

Hot rodders liked the design of the '57 Chev. Still, the hot rodders made improvements to it.

In 1963, Pontiac began to sell factory-made hot rods. John DeLorean, a young General Motors employee, designed the Pontiac GTO. It was the first **muscle car**, meaning a car with a large stock engine and custom detailing.

Muscle cars began to catch on. Throughout the 1960s, all of the three major American car makers designed and built these ready-made

makers designed and built these ready-made hot rods.

Hot Rodding Continues

Despite the increase of **ready-made** muscle cars of the 1960s, hot rodders continued to design their own machines. Today, hot rodders build the most popular hot rods from Ford Coupes, 1949 Mercuries, and 1957 Chevrolets.

Avid hot rodders still bore their cylinders. They still add superchargers and swap engines.

They also exchange ideas at organized hot rod shows and races. Thanks to the National Hot Rod Association (NHRA), these events attract hot rodders. Each year, thousands of spectators gather to admire the beautiful and powerful machines.

Glossary

blower–a supercharger that forces fuel into an engine

bore–to make a cylinder larger by grinding it

carburetor–mixes gasoline and air before the valves suck the mixture into the engine

chopped–a car roof that a hot rodder has lowered several inches

chrome–a very shiny silver metal

customize–to change a car according to an owner's needs and tastes

cylinder–can-shaped area of an engine where air and gasoline explode

detailing–custom work done to visible parts of a hot rod

deuce coupe–a Ford from the 1920s or 1930s that seats only a driver and passenger

driveshaft–a long rod that connects a car's wheels to the pistons. As the pistons spin the rod, the rod spins the wheels.

dual carburetors–two carburetors on one engine

engine block–solid piece of metal that holds a car's cylinders

engine swapping–to take a different and more powerful engine from one car and put it into another

fiberglass–plastic-like material made of small glass fibers

flathead Ford–early four-cylinder Ford engines

Fordillac–a Ford coupe with a Cadillac engine

fuel–a mix of gasoline and air that powers an engine

fuel injector–a device that squirts a perfect mixture of gasoline and air into an engine

hop-up–to give a car more power

hot rodder–a person who builds and drives hot rods

internal combustion engine–an engine that propels a car by creating an explosion of gasoline and air inside a can-shaped cylinder

metallic–a kind of paint that contains tiny glittering metal chips

muscle–another word for a car's power

muscle car–a car with a large stock engine and custom body parts

Model A–popular Ford car built in the 1920s and 1930s. Model A's are still popular with hot rodders

Model T–Ford's first car, the first mass-produced automobile

National Hot Rod Association (NHRA)–group formed to promote drag racing

pearlescent–a kind of paint whose finish looks like the glow of a pearl

pinstriping–a kind of detailing in which painters hand-paint thin stripes onto a hot rod's body

piston–a solid cylinder that moves inside a larger, hollow cylinder

Shoebox Ford–nickname for a 1949 Mercury with a chopped roof

Southern California Timing Association (SCTA)–group formed to organize hot rod races and shows

stock–a car's part that workers put on in the factory

supercharger–device that blows fuel into an engine

suspension–a system that allows a car to ride smoothly

tuck-and-roll–fancy hand-sewn upholstery

V-8–an engine with eight cylinders placed in the shape of the letter "V"

valve–opening through which gasoline and air enter a cylinder. A valve is also an opening through which exhaust escapes the cylinder.

whitewalls–tires with wide white rings on the sides

To Learn More

Fetherston, David A. *Heroes of Hot Rodding.* Osceola, WI: Motorbooks International, 1992.

Knudson, Richard L. *Restroring Yesterday's Cars.* Minneapolis, MN: Lerner Publications Company, 1983

Ready, Kirk L. Custom Cars. Minneapolis, MN: Lerner Publications Company, 1982.

Sutton, Richard. *Car, Eyewitness Books.* New York, NY: Alfred A. Knopf, 1990.

Hot Rod **Magazine**

Some Useful Addresses

Historical Automobile Society of Canada
14 Elizabeth Street
Guelph, Ontario N1E 2X2

National Hot Rod Association (NHRA)
2035 Financial Way
Glendora, CA 91740

National Street Rod Association
3041 Getwell
Memphis, TN 38118

Vintage Car Club of Canada
P.O. Box 3070
Vancouver, British Columbia

Photo Credits:
©Petersen Publishing Company: pgs. 5, 6, 9, 10-11, 12, 13, 14, 15, 16, 18-19, 23, 24-25, 28, 30, 32, 34-35, 37, 38, 40.
©Peter Ford: pgs. 20, 26, 31.

Index